I So Totally Got This

KNOCK
KNOCK®
LOS ANGELES, CALIFORNIA

Created, published, and distributed by Knock Knock
11111 Jefferson Blvd. #5167
Culver City, CA 90231
knockknockstuff.com
Knock Knock is a registered trademark of Knock Knock LLC
Inner-Truth is a registered trademark of Knock Knock LLC

ISBN: 978-1-68349-282-5
UPC: 825703-50196-4

10 9 8 7 6 5 4 3

I SO GOT THIS.

I so got this. I so don't got this. Nope. Let's try this again. I so totally got this! Much better.

No matter what you do and how good you are, you're going to doubt yourself sometimes. Everyone has self-doubts. The key to being successful is to take note of these and climb right on over them, reminding yourself that you're hot stuff and you can do whatever you set your mind to.

We know, easier said than done.

Sometimes, what you really need to do is fake it. Tell yourself you've got it. Tell everyone else you've got it. They won't be the wiser. In the end, most of the time, you will find that you do indeed "got it." And if you drop it? No big deal. Just say, "I meant to do that!" and pick it back up.

We're not the first to argue that self-confidence will take you far, even when you're not sure you have the chops or guts to achieve something. Great thinkers and successful people have been saying this for centuries. The Roman poet Virgil wrote: "They succeed, because they think they can." Samuel Johnson wrote an entire dictionary in the 1700s that took him nearly a decade and had an enormous impact on the English language. How did he do it? As he wrote, "Self-confidence is the first requisite to great undertakings." Theodore Roosevelt also asserted it: "Believe you can and you're halfway there."

Psychologists agree. *Psychology Today* asserts, "You can start to build your confidence right now by telling yourself that you've got it in you; the more you believe that you are capable, the more you will be." Mark Leary, professor of psychology and neuroscience at Duke University, calls this "self-efficacy"—the belief that you can do what you set out to do. With self-efficacy, you'll step out of your comfort zone to try new things, you'll keep going even when meeting obstacles, and you'll rebound when things don't go as you'd hoped.

And it's not just you who will be convinced. If you seem self-assured, if it looks like you believe in yourself, people around you will believe it, too. In a research project on the effects of projecting confidence, business professors Gavin Kilduff and Adam Galinksy demonstrated that the way you present yourself to people when you first encounter them will affect your long-term status in a group. If you appear assertive, confident, and more able, you will be more highly regarded by the group going forward. In short, they'll marvel at your got-it-togetherness, whether it's real or imagined.

Interestingly, the participants in Kilduff and Galinsky's study who exhibited the most confidence were those who had done a writing exercise before joining the group, expounding on their ambitions and aspirations. That is, journaling was a key tool in boosting their confidence. Of course, we're not surprised. Journaling is a great companion as you work on your poise and learn to quell self-doubt.

As celebrated self-help author Deepak Chopra claims, "Journaling is one of the most powerful tools we have to transform our lives." According to a widely cited study by James W. Pennebaker and Janel D. Seagal, "Writing about important personal experiences in an emotional way ... brings about improvements in mental and physical health." Proven benefits include better stress management, strengthened immune systems, fewer doctor visits, and improvement in chronic illnesses such as asthma.

It's not entirely clear how journaling accomplishes all this. Catharsis is involved, but many also point to the value of organizing experiences into a cohesive narrative. According to *Newsweek*, some experts believe that journaling "forces us to transform the ruminations cluttering our minds into coherent stories." In many ways, journaling enables us to see beyond doubt and uncertainty so that we can focus on our hopes and aspirations as well as the skills and talents that will take us where we want to go.

Specialists agree that in order to reap the benefits of journaling you should do it quasi-daily, for as little as five minutes at a time (though at least fifteen minutes is best), even on the days when you're not doubting anything. Finding regular writing times and comfortable locations can help with consistency. If you find yourself unable to rise above "I ain't got it," don't stress. Instead, use the quotes inside this journal as a jumping-off point for observations and explorations.

What should you write about? The journal is your oyster. Write about what you want to accomplish, whether or not you think it's realistic. Note what you'd need to do to get there. Acknowledge your strengths. Record the qualities of self-assured people you admire. Write about times you missed the mark and what you could do to fix it. Write about the situations when you did really nail it, no faking involved. Be your best and loudest cheerleader. Write whatever comes, and don't criticize it; journaling is a means of self-reflection, not a structured composition. In other words, spew. Finally, determine a safe home for your journal where you can find it easily, on days when you've knocked it out of the park and days when you couldn't get a single hit. Keep it by your bed, near the fridge, or wherever you keep your sports metaphors.

And you might as well kick off that whole believing in yourself deal this very moment. As actor Hugh Laurie points out, "There's almost no such thing as ready. There's only now. And you may as well do it now. I mean, I say that confidently as if I'm about to go bungee jumping or something—I'm not. I'm not a crazed risk taker. But I do think that, generally speaking, now is as good a time as any." After all, you so got this. You really do. Right?

The best motto for a long march is "Don't grumble. Plug on." You hold your future in your own hands.

Sir Frederick Treves

Why I So Totally Got This Today:

LEVEL OF CONFIDENCE IN ACTUALLY NAILING IT:

□ **?**　　　□ **!**　　　□ **!!**　　　□ **!!!**

You have brains in your head. You have feet in your shoes. You can steer yourself in any direction you choose.

Dr. Seuss

Why I So Totally Got This Today:

Opportunities are rarely offered; they're seized.

Sheryl Sandberg

Why I So Totally Got This Today:

....

....

....

....

....

....

....

....

....

....

....

....

....

LEVEL OF CONFIDENCE IN ACTUALLY NAILING IT:

□ **?**　　　□ **!**　　　□ **!!**　　　□ **!!!**

Without leaps of imagination, or dreaming, we lose the excitement of possibilities. Dreaming, after all, is a form of planning.

Gloria Steinem

Why I So Totally Got This Today:

We work in the dark—we do what we can—we give what we have. Our doubt is our passion and our passion is our task.

Henry James

Why I So Totally Got This Today:

LEVEL OF CONFIDENCE IN ACTUALLY NAILING IT:

☐ **?**   ☐ **!**   ☐ **!!**   ☐ **!!!**

Got nothing to prove, but I'ma show you how I do

 Lizzo

DATE:

Why I So Totally Got This Today:

LEVEL OF CONFIDENCE IN ACTUALLY NAILING IT:

□ ? □ ! □ !! □ !!!

You can do anything you want in life if you dress for it.

Edith Head

Why I So Totally Got This Today:

Life loves to be taken by the lapel and told: "I'm with you kid. Let's go."

Maya Angelou

Why I So Totally Got This Today:

LEVEL OF CONFIDENCE IN ACTUALLY NAILING IT:

□ **?**　　□ **!**　　□ **!!**　　□ **!\!**

Get the thing done and let them howl.

Nellie McClung

Why I So Totally Got This Today:

The Sun himself is weak when he first rises, and gathers strength and courage as the day gets on.

Charles Dickens

Why I So Totally Got This Today:

....

....

....

....

....

....

....

....

....

....

....

LEVEL OF CONFIDENCE IN ACTUALLY NAILING IT:

□ **?**   □ **!**   □ **!!**   □ **!!!**

Where you tend a rose, my lad, A thistle cannot grow.

Frances Hodgson Burnett

Why I So Totally Got This Today:

LEVEL OF CONFIDENCE IN ACTUALLY NAILING IT:

□ **?**　　　□ **!**　　　□ **!!**　　　□ **!!!**

Don't you worry about me. I'll always come out on top.

Astrid Lindgren

Why I So Totally Got This Today:

LEVEL OF CONFIDENCE IN ACTUALLY NAILING IT:

□ **?** □ **!** □ **!!** □ **!!!**

Nobody beats Vitas Gerulaitis seventeen times in a row.

Why I So Totally Got This Today:

LEVEL OF CONFIDENCE IN ACTUALLY NAILING IT:

☐ ? ☐ ! ☐ !! ☐ !!!

I know very little about acting. I'm just an incredibly gifted faker.

Robert Downey Jr.

Why I So Totally Got This Today:

LEVEL OF CONFIDENCE IN ACTUALLY NAILING IT:

□ **?**   □ **!**   □ **!!**   □ **!!!**

I am the master of my fate,

I am the captain of my soul.

William Ernest Henley

Why I So Totally Got This Today:

Sometimes you just have to put on lip gloss and pretend to be psyched.

Mindy Kaling

Why I So Totally Got This Today:

LEVEL OF CONFIDENCE IN ACTUALLY NAILING IT:

□ **?**   □ **!**   □ **!!**   □ **!!!**

Do. Or do not. There is no try.

Yoda

Why I So Totally Got This Today:

I have discovered in life that there are ways of getting almost anywhere you want to go, if you really want to go.

Langston Hughes

Why I So Totally Got This Today:

If you don't place your foot on the rope, you'll never cross the chasm.

Liz Smith

Why I So Totally Got This Today:

LEVEL OF CONFIDENCE IN ACTUALLY NAILING IT:

□ **?**　　　□ **!**　　　□ **!!**　　　□ **!!!**

I was amazed that what I needed to survive could be carried on my back. And, most surprising of all, that I could carry it.

Cheryl Strayed

— Why I So Totally Got This Today: —

LEVEL OF CONFIDENCE IN ACTUALLY NAILING IT:

□ ? □ ! □ ‼ □ ⫶!

You can't be that kid standing at the top of the waterslide, overthinking it. You have to go down the chute.

Tina Fey

— Why I So Totally Got This Today: —

LEVEL OF CONFIDENCE IN ACTUALLY NAILING IT:

□ ?   □ !   □ !!   □ !!!

Don't stop believin'
Hold on to the feelin'

Journey

Why I So Totally Got This Today:

You can't connect the dots looking forward; you can only connect them looking backward. So you have to trust that the dots will somehow connect in your future.

Steve Jobs

Why I So Totally Got This Today:

LEVEL OF CONFIDENCE IN ACTUALLY NAILING IT:

□ **?**　　　□ **!**　　　□ **!!**　　　□ **!!!**

I spoke without fear of contradiction. I had done nothing to prove my position. But I simply did not suffer from self-doubt.

Elia Kazan

── Why I So Totally Got This Today: ──

Beware; for I am fearless, and therefore powerful.

Mary Wollstonecraft Shelley

— Why I So Totally Got This Today: —

LEVEL OF CONFIDENCE IN ACTUALLY NAILING IT:

□ **?**   □ **!**   □ **!!**   □ **!!!**

Let everything happen to you: beauty and terror. Only press on: no feeling is final.

Rainer Maria Rilke

Why I So Totally Got This Today:

LEVEL OF CONFIDENCE IN ACTUALLY NAILING IT:

□ ? □ ! □ !! □ !!!

All life is an experiment. The more experiments you make, the better… What if you do fail, & get fairly rolled in the dirt once or twice? Up again, you shall never more be so afraid of a tumble.

Ralph Waldo Emerson

Why I So Totally Got This Today:

LEVEL OF CONFIDENCE IN ACTUALLY NAILING IT:

□ ? □ ! □ ‼ □ ‼

She must find a boat and sail in it. No guarantee of shore. Only a conviction that what she wanted could exist, if she dared to find it.

Jeanette Winterson

Why I So Totally Got This Today:

LEVEL OF CONFIDENCE IN ACTUALLY NAILING IT:

□ ?   □ !   □ !!   □ !!!

When we own our stories, we get to write the ending.

Brené Brown

Why I So Totally Got This Today:

LEVEL OF CONFIDENCE IN ACTUALLY NAILING IT:

☐ **?**　　☐ **!**　　☐ **!!**　　☐ **!!!**

We are the ones we've been waiting for. We are the change that we seek.

Barack Obama

Why I So Totally Got This Today:

This is the fast lane, folks... and some of us like it here.

Hunter S. Thompson

Why I So Totally Got This Today:

LEVEL OF CONFIDENCE IN ACTUALLY NAILING IT:

□ ?   □ !   □ !!   □ !!!

Life is always a tightrope or a feather bed. Give me the tightrope.

Edith Wharton

Why I So Totally Got This Today:

LEVEL OF CONFIDENCE IN ACTUALLY NAILING IT:

□ **?**   □ **!**   □ **!!**   □ **!!!**

No matter what happens, if I get pushed down, I'm going to come right back up.

Why I So Totally Got This Today:

LEVEL OF CONFIDENCE IN ACTUALLY NAILING IT:

□ **?**   □ **!**   □ **!!**   □ **!!!**

My passions were all gathered together like fingers that made a fist.

 Bette Davis

Why I So Totally Got This Today:

LEVEL OF CONFIDENCE IN ACTUALLY NAILING IT:

□ **?**   □ **!**   □ **!!**   □ **!!!**

A quilt may take a year, but if you just keep doing it, you get a quilt.

Chuck Close

Why I So Totally Got This Today:

Perseverance is a great element of success. If you only knock long enough and loud enough at the gate, you are sure to wake up somebody.

Henry Wadsworth Longfellow

Why I So Totally Got This Today:

LEVEL OF CONFIDENCE IN ACTUALLY NAILING IT:

□ ?   □ !   □ !!   □ !!!

Who climbs with toil, wheresoe'er, Shall find wings waiting there.

Henry Charles Beeching

Why I So Totally Got This Today:

LEVEL OF CONFIDENCE IN ACTUALLY NAILING IT:

□ **?**　　　□ **!**　　　□ **!!**　　　□ **!!!**

A dame that knows the ropes isn't likely to get tied up.

Mae West

Why I So Totally Got This Today:

LEVEL OF CONFIDENCE IN ACTUALLY NAILING IT:

□ **?**   □ **!**   □ **!!**   □ **!!!**

The one thing that you have that nobody else has is you. Your voice, your mind, your story, your vision. So write and draw and build and play and dance and live as only you can.

Neil Gaiman

Why I So Totally Got This Today:

LEVEL OF CONFIDENCE IN ACTUALLY NAILING IT:

□ **?**   □ **!**   □ **!!**   □ **!/!**

Tough times never last, but tough people do!

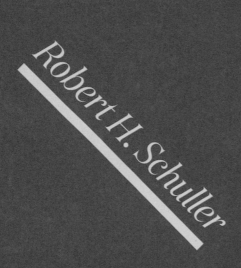

Robert H. Schuller

Why I So Totally Got This Today:

Vitality shows in not only the ability to persist but the ability to start over.

F. Scott Fitzgerald

Why I So Totally Got This Today:

Woe-is-me is not an attractive narrative.

Maureen Dowd

Why I So Totally Got This Today:

What seem to us bitter trials are often blessings in disguise.

Oscar Wilde

Why I So Totally Got This Today:

LEVEL OF CONFIDENCE IN ACTUALLY NAILING IT:

□ **?**   □ **!**   □ **!!**   □ **!!!**

It is a common experience that a problem difficult at night is resolved in the morning after the committee of sleep has worked on it.

John Steinbeck

Why I So Totally Got This Today:

LEVEL OF CONFIDENCE IN ACTUALLY NAILING IT:

☐ **?**　　　☐ **!**　　　☐ **!!**　　　☐ **!\!**

I like breakfast-time better than any other moment in the day... No dust has settled on one's mind then, and it presents a clear mirror to the rays of things.

George Eliot

Why I So Totally Got This Today:

LEVEL OF CONFIDENCE IN ACTUALLY NAILING IT:

□ ? □ ! □ !! □ !!!

It is the same with people as it is with riding a bike. Only when moving can one comfortably maintain one's balance.

Albert Einstein

Why I So Totally Got This Today:

I feel pretty

Oh, so pretty

That the city should give
me its key.

A committee

Should be organized to
honor me.

Stephen Sondheim

Why I So Totally Got This Today:

LEVEL OF CONFIDENCE IN ACTUALLY NAILING IT:

□ ?   □ /   □ !/   □ /!/

Fearlessness is not the absence of fear. Rather, it's the mastery of fear.

Arianna Huffington

Why I So Totally Got This Today:

LEVEL OF CONFIDENCE IN ACTUALLY NAILING IT:

☐ **?**   ☐ **!**   ☐ **!!**   ☐ **!!!**

It's okay is a cosmic truth.

Richard Bach

Why I So Totally Got This Today:

LEVEL OF CONFIDENCE IN ACTUALLY NAILING IT:

□ **?**   □ **!**   □ **!!**   □ **!!!**

As you get older you're not afraid of doubt. Doubt isn't running the show. You take out all the self-agonizing.

Clint Eastwood

Why I So Totally Got This Today:

LEVEL OF CONFIDENCE IN ACTUALLY NAILING IT:

□ **?**　　　□ **!**　　　□ **!!**　　　□ **!!!**

Stay aware, listen carefully, and yell for help if you need it.

Judy Blume

Why I So Totally Got This Today:

LEVEL OF CONFIDENCE IN ACTUALLY NAILING IT:

□ **?**　　　□ **!**　　　□ **!!**　　　□ **!!!**

I can't think of anyone I admire who isn't fueled by self-doubt. It's an essential ingredient. It's the grit in the oyster.

Richard Eyre

Why I So Totally Got This Today:

LEVEL OF CONFIDENCE IN ACTUALLY NAILING IT:

□ ? □ ! □ !! □ !!!

A career is built one paragraph at a time.

Barbara Kingsolver

Why I So Totally Got This Today:

....

....

....

....

....

....

....

....

....

....

....

....

....

....

LEVEL OF CONFIDENCE IN ACTUALLY NAILING IT:

□ **?**   □ **/**   □ **!!**   □ **!!!**

Above all, be the heroine of your life, not the victim.

Nora Ephron

Why I So Totally Got This Today:

I am so smart. I am so smart. I am so smart. I am so smart. S-M-R-T—I mean S-M-A-R-T.

Homer Simpson

— Why I So Totally Got This Today: —

LEVEL OF CONFIDENCE IN ACTUALLY NAILING IT:

□ **?**   □ **!**   □ **!!**   □ **!!!**

I was someone with not much self-belief at all and yet in this one thing in my life I believed. That was the one thing in my life. I felt "I can tell a story."

J. K. Rowling

Why I So Totally Got This Today:

LEVEL OF CONFIDENCE IN ACTUALLY NAILING IT:

☐ **?**   ☐ **!**   ☐ **!!**   ☐ **!!!**

There's not a thing wrong with you, you're right all the way through.

Emma Donoghue

Why I So Totally Got This Today:

LEVEL OF CONFIDENCE IN ACTUALLY NAILING IT:

□ **?**   □ **!**   □ **!!**   □ **!!!**

I am a champion and you're gonna hear me roar.

Katy Perry

Why I So Totally Got This Today:

LEVEL OF CONFIDENCE IN ACTUALLY NAILING IT:

☐ ?   ☐ !   ☐ !!   ☐ !!!

When all else fails, you always have delusion.

Conan O'Brien

Why I So Totally Got This Today:

LEVEL OF CONFIDENCE IN ACTUALLY NAILING IT:

☐ **?**   ☐ **!**   ☐ **!!**   ☐ **!!!**

Let other pens dwell on guilt and misery.

Jane Austen

— Why I So Totally Got This Today: —

LEVEL OF CONFIDENCE IN ACTUALLY NAILING IT:

□ **?**　　　□ **/**　　　□ **!/**　　　□ **/!/**

God knows, there's enough to worry about without worrying about worrying about things.

Edward Gorey

Why I So Totally Got This Today:

....

....

....

....

....

....

....

....

....

....

....

....

....

LEVEL OF CONFIDENCE IN ACTUALLY NAILING IT:

□ **?**   □ **!**   □ **!!**   □ **!!!**

Leave it to me: I'm always top banana in the shock department.

Truman Capote

Why I So Totally Got This Today:

LEVEL OF CONFIDENCE IN ACTUALLY NAILING IT:

☐ **?**   ☐ **!**   ☐ **!!**   ☐ **!!!**

Every day is a new beginning and a chance to blow it.

Cathy Guisewite

Why I So Totally Got This Today:

And the trouble is, if you don't risk anything, you risk even *more.*

Erica Jong

Why I So Totally Got This Today:

It's a good thing to have all
the props pulled out from
under us occasionally.
It gives us some sense of
what is rock under our
feet, and what is sand.

Madeleine L'Engle

Why I So Totally Got This Today:

LEVEL OF CONFIDENCE IN ACTUALLY NAILING IT:

□ **?**   □ **!**   □ **!!**   □ **!!!**

Courage is being scared to death— and saddling up anyway.

John Wayne

Why I So Totally Got This Today:

LEVEL OF CONFIDENCE IN ACTUALLY NAILING IT:

☐ ?   ☐ !   ☐ !!   ☐ !!!

Life is either a daring adventure or nothing.

Helen Keller

Why I So Totally Got This Today:

LEVEL OF CONFIDENCE IN ACTUALLY NAILING IT:

□ ? □ ! □ !! □ !!!

Failure isn't the enemy—fear is. One learns, after all, by failing. This is elementary; we all know it, except when it applies to ourselves.

Carla Needleman

Why I So Totally Got This Today:

LEVEL OF CONFIDENCE IN ACTUALLY NAILING IT:

□ **?**　　　□ **!**　　　□ **!!**　　　□ **!!!**

Make it work.

Tim Gunn

Why I So Totally Got This Today:

When asked, "How do you write?" I invariably answer, "One word at a time."

Stephen King

Why I So Totally Got This Today:

LEVEL OF CONFIDENCE IN ACTUALLY NAILING IT:

□ **?**   □ **!**   □ **!!**   □ **!!!**

Be strong, be brave, be true. Endure.

Dave Eggers

Why I So Totally Got This Today:

LEVEL OF CONFIDENCE IN ACTUALLY NAILING IT:

☐ ?   ☐ !   ☐ !!   ☐ !!!

If you have the guts to be yourself... other people'll pay your price.

John Updike

Why I So Totally Got This Today:

You need to learn how to select your thoughts just the same way you select what clothes you're gonna wear every day. This is a power you can cultivate.

Elizabeth Gilbert

Why I So Totally Got This Today:

LEVEL OF CONFIDENCE IN ACTUALLY NAILING IT:

□ ?   □ !   □ !!   □ !!!

The world is a wheel, and it will all come round right.

Benjamin Disraeli

Why I So Totally Got This Today:

....
....
....
....
....
....
....
....
....
....
....
....

LEVEL OF CONFIDENCE IN ACTUALLY NAILING IT:

☐ ?   ☐ !   ☐ !!   ☐ !!!

I think there should be a rule that everyone in the world should get a standing ovation at least once in their lives.

R. J. Palacio

Why I So Totally Got This Today:

LEVEL OF CONFIDENCE IN ACTUALLY NAILING IT:

☐ ?   ☐ !   ☐ !!   ☐ !!!

Bunkum and tummyrot! You'll never get anywhere if you go about what-iffing like that...We want no whatiffers around here.

Roald Dahl

Why I So Totally Got This Today:

LEVEL OF CONFIDENCE IN ACTUALLY NAILING IT:

□ **?**　　　□ **!**　　　□ **!!**　　　□ **!!!**

Trust yourself. You know more than you think you do.

Dr. Benjamin Spock

Why I So Totally Got This Today:

....

....

....

....

....

....

....

....

....

....

....

....

LEVEL OF CONFIDENCE IN ACTUALLY NAILING IT:

☐ **?**　　☐ **!**　　☐ **!!**　　☐ **!\!**

Yup. Nailed it.

Knock Knock